Wolfgang Amadeus Mozart

PIANO CONCERTOS
Nos. 23-27
In Full Score

with Mozart's Cadenzas for Nos. 23 and 27
and the Concert Rondo in D

Wolfgang Amadeus Mozart

PIANO CONCERTOS
Nos. 23-27
In Full Score

with Mozart's Cadenzas for Nos. 23 and 27
and the Concert Rondo in D

From the Breitkopf & Härtel
Complete Works Edition

Dover Publications, Inc.
New York

Published in Canada by General Publishing Company, Ltd.,
30 Lesmill Road, Don Mills, Toronto, Ontario.
Published in the United Kingdom by Constable and
Company, Ltd., 10 Orange Street, London WC2H 7EG.

This Dover edition, first published in 1978, is a republication of portions of *Serie 16 (Concerte für das Pianoforte)* of *Wolfgang Amadeus Mozart's Werke. Kritisch durchgesehene Gesammtausgabe,* originally published by Breitkopf & Härtel, Leipzig, 1877–1879. The specific portions included here, comprising the complete Piano Concertos Nos. 23–27, appeared in 1879. To these have been added the cadenzas for Nos. 23 and 27, extracted from *Serie 22 (Kleinere Stücke für das Pianoforte)* of the same general work, as published in 1878.

International Standard Book Number: 0-486-23600-5
Library of Congress Catalog Card Number: 77-15719

Manufactured in the United States of America
Dover Publications, Inc.
180 Varick Street
New York, N.Y. 10014

Contents

Note: The concerto numbers given here, those of the *Gesammtausgabe,* are still in general use. Cuthbert Girdlestone, however, in his important study *Mozart and His Piano Concertos,* does not recognize four early works as true concertos and numbers the five concertos included here as Nos. 19–23, respectively. All the cadenzas collectively have the Köchel number 624.

Note: The W.A.M. numbers at the foot of each page are the same as the Köchel numbers for the respective compositions.

Piano Concerto No. 23 in A Major, K.488

p
p
p
Vcl.
p
Bassi
p

cresc.
cresc.
cresc.
f
cresc.
cresc.
cresc.
f
p
SOLO
p

TUTTI
SOLO
f
a 2.
legato
p
sf
tr

sf
p
sf a 2.
f
dolce
p

p
p
p
legato

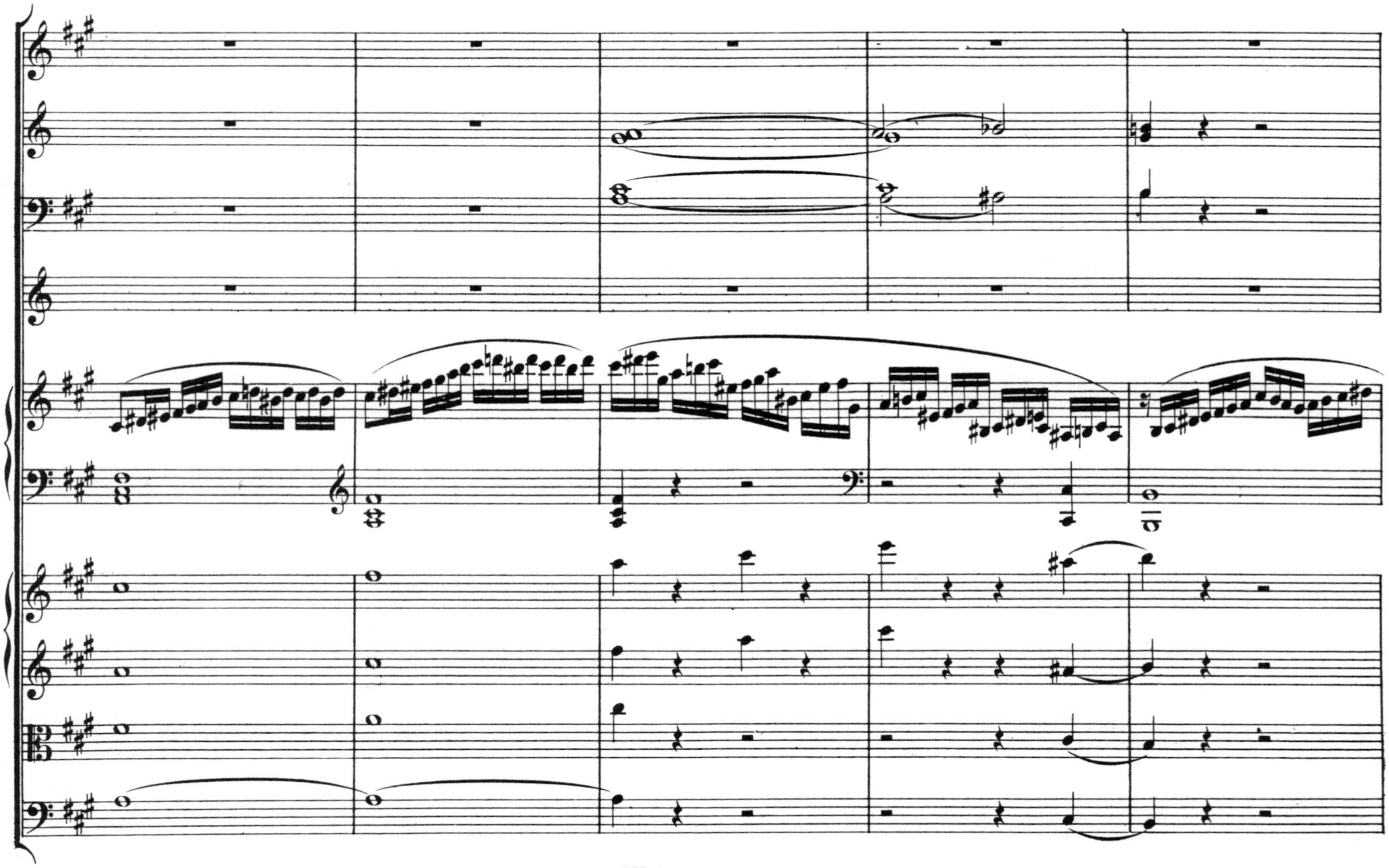

TUTTI
a 2.
tr
SOLO

TUTTI
SOLO
p
p
p
p
TUTTI
SOLO

TUTTI
SOLO
legato

TUTTI
SOLO
p
TUTTI
SOLO

TUTTI
p
p
p
p

SOLO
TUTTI
f
a 2.

SOLO
legato
p
p
p
p
f
p
f
p
f
p
fp

legato

Clar.
Fag.
tr
legato
Clar.
Fag.
Cor.

TUTTI
cresc.
a 2.
f
p
tr

TUTTI
SOLO
tr
Cadenza

a 2.
tr
Andante.
SOLO
TUTTI

SOLO
f
f
f
f
f
f
f
p
p
p
p

TUTTI
SOLO

TUTTI
SOLO
TUTTI

SOLO
a 2.
legato

p
p
p
p
pizz.
pizz.
pizz.
pizz.
arco
arco
arco
arco

pp
Presto.
SOLO
TUTTI
f
p

Clar.
Fag.
a 2.
a 2.

a 2.
SOLO

Clar.
TUTTI
p
Cor.
p
SOLO
p
p
p
p

Fl.
TUTTI
p
Fag.
p
SOLO
legato
Fl.
p
Clar.
p
Fag.
p

a 2.
p

Vcl.
Bassi
tr

Vcl.
a 2.
legato
tr
pizz.
pizz.
pizz.

Bassi
p
arco
arco
arco

TUTTI

a 2.
a 2.
SOLO
legato
p
p
p
p

TUTTI
SOLO
a 2.
p
legato
f
p
TUTTI
p

SOLO
legato
legato
legato

Clar.
Fag.
legato

TUTTI
Solo

TUTTI
TUTTI
SOLO
SOLO
legato

legato
Vcl.
Bassi

Vcl.
legato
a 2.
pizz.
pizz.
pizz.

legato
Bassi
p
arco
arco
arco

TUTTI

SOLO
p
legato

TUTTI
f
a 2.
SOLO
a 2.
p
legato
pizz.
p
pizz.
p
pizz.
p
p

TUTTI
arco
arco
arco
SOLO

TUTTI
SOLO
a 2.
TUTTI
a 2.

Piano Concerto No. 24 in C Minor, K.491

f

I.
p
Fl.
Ob.
Fag.
I.

I.
p
I.
a 2.
f

I.
I.
I.
a 2.
Vcl.
Basso
Bassi
Vcl.
Bassi

SOLO.
p
f
tr

TUTTI.
SOLO.
a 2.

legato
Ob.
TUTTI.
Clar.
Fag.
Cor.
p

SOLO.
legato
Fl.
I.
I.
I.

Fl.
Ob.
Clar.

TUTTI.
I.
p
I.
p
I.
p
p
p
p
p

SOLO.
Cl.
Fag.
Cor.
Vcl.
Bassi
Fl.
Cl.
Fag.
Cor.

Fl.
Clar.
Fag.
I.
legato
Fl.
Ob.
I.
Clar.
Fag.
p
p
p
p

Fl.
p
Ob.
p
Clar.
p
Fag.
p
Cor.
p
legato

Fl.
Cor.
Fl.
Ob.
Clar.
Fag.
Cor.
TUTTI.
cresc.
f

SOLO.
p

Fl.
Cl.
Fag.
I.
p
Ob.
TUTTI.
SOLO.
Clar.
Fag.
f
legato
p

Fl.
Ob.
Clar.
Fag.
tr

TUTTI.
SOLO.
f

TUTTI.
SOLO.
TUTTI.
Fl.
Ob.
Clar.
Fag.
Cor.
SOLO.
TUTTI.
SOLO.

Fl.
Ob.
Clar.
Fag.
Cor.
p
tr

I.
I.
legato
TUTTI.
a 2.
fp
p
f

Fl.
SOLO.
Ob.
Clar.
Fag.
p
p
p
p

I.
I.

SOLO.
Fl.
Ob.
Clar.
Fag.
I.
Cor.
Ob.
Clar.
Fag.
Vcl.
Bassi

Ob.
Clar.
Fag.
Cor.
legato
Ob.
Clar.
Fag.
I

Fl.
Ob.
Clar.
Fag.
legato.
Fl.
Ob.
I.
Fag.

Ob.
I.
Fag.
Fl.
Ob.
Fag.
Fl.
Ob.
Clar.
Fag.
I.
p

TUTTI.
I.
I.
SOLO.
Cor.
legato

Fl.
Ob.
Clar.
tr
cresc.
cresc.
cresc.
TUTTI.
f
a 2.

a 2.
a 2.
Cadenza
a 2.
Vcl.
Bassi

SOLO.
legato

Tr.
Timp.
tr
pp
a 2.

Larghetto.

SOLO.
TUTTI.
Flauto.
Oboi.
Clarinetti in B.
Fagotti.
Corni in Es.
Pianoforte.
legato
Violino I.
Violino II.
Viola.
Violoncello e Basso.
SOLO.

Ob.
Clar.
Fag.
Fl.
TUTTI.
Fl.
Ob.
SOLO.

p
p
p
p
Fl.
TUTTI.
Ob.
Fag.
Fl.
Ob.
Fag.

SOLO.
Fl.
p
Ob.
p
Clar.
p
Fag.
p
Cor.
p
TUTTI.

Fl.
SOLO.
Clar.
Fag.
Cor.
p
p
p
p

Fl.
TUTTI.
Clar.
Fag.
Cor.
SOLO.

Ob.
TUTTI.
Clar.
Fag.
Cor.
SOLO.

Ob.
Clar.
Fag.

TUTTI.
Cor I.
Cor II.
SOLO.

Allegretto.
TUTTI.
Flauto.
Oboi.
Clarinetti in B.
a 2.
Fagotti.
Corni in Es.
Trombe in C.
Timpani in C. G.
Pianoforte.
Violino I.
Violino II.
Viola.
Violoncello e Basso.
Allegretto.
1.

2.
SOLO.
Fl.
Ob.
Clar.
Fag.
Cor.
2.
1.
2.
1.
2.
Ob.
1.
2.
TUTTI
1.
2.

SOLO.
Fl.
Ob.
Clar.
Fag.
legato
Ob.
Clar.
Fag.
TUTTI.

Fl.
Ob.
Clar.
Fag.
SOLO.
legato

legato
Fl.
Ob.
Clar.
Fag.
f
TUTTI.
a2.
f

SOLO.
a 2.
legato

TUTTI.
Fl.
Ob.
Clar.
Cor.
a 2.

Cl.
Fag.
Cor.
Clar.
SOLO.
Fag.
Cor.

TUTTI.
Clar.
Fag.
Cor.
sfp

sfp
sfp
sfp
sfp
legato
legato

legato
Ob.
TUTTI.
I.
Fl.
Ob.
Fag.
I.

SOLO.
Ob.
Fag.
TUTTI.

Fl.
Ob.
Fag.
SOLO.

Fl.
Ob.
Fag.

Fl.
Ob.
Clar.
Fag.

Cadenza

Fl.
Ob.
Clar.
Fag.
I.
I.
legato

Fl.
Clar.
I.
Fag.
Fl.
Ob.
I.

I.
TUTTI.
a 2.
a 2.
a 2.

Piano Concerto No. 25 in C Major, K.503

I.
a 2.
a 2.

a 2.
a 2.

a 2.
p
Fl.
Ob.
Fag.
p
p
p
p
p

p
p
p
p
a 2.
p
a 2.
p
p
Fl.
Ob.
Fag.
Cor.

cresc.
f
a 2.
p
SOLO
tr
legato

Fl.
Ob.
Fag.
Cor.
p

TUTTI
SOLO
a 2.

Ob.
Fag.
legato
Fag.
Cor.
p
p

TUTTI
a 2.
SOLO
legato

p
mf
Fl.
Ob.
6
Fag.
a 2.
Cor.
legato

legato
Vcl.
Ob.
Fag.
I.
I.
legato
Bassi
Fl.
Vcl.
Bassi

Fl.
Ob.
Fag.
I.
legato
Fag.
tr

TUTTI
SOLO
TUTTI
SOLO

Fl.
TUTTI
cresc.
tr
f
a 2.

a 2.

SOLO
p
legato
p
p
p
p
Fl.
Ob.
Fag.
a 2.
p
p
p
3
3
3
3

TUTTI
I.
a 2.
a 2.
SOLO
I.
I.

Fl.
Ob.
Fag.
p
p
p
p

p
legato
a 2.

TUTTI
SOLO
f
p
tr
legato

p
I.
legato
I.
6
6

p
p
TUTTI
SOLO
f
a 2.

legato
p
p
p
p
3

Fl.
Ob. I.
p
p
legato
Vcl.
Bassi
Fl.
Ob. I.
Fag. I.
p
Bassi
Vcl.

p
I.
p
p
tr
Bassi
legato

Fag.
a 2.
Cor.
legato
tr
TUTTI
SOLO
Fl.
Ob.
Fag.
tr
tr

Cor.
Fl.
Ob.
Fag.
Cor.
I.
cresc.
cresc.
cresc.
f
tr

TUTTI
a 2.
a 2.
Cadenza
tr

a 2.
a 2.

a 2.
cresc.
f
p

Andante.
TUTTI
Flauto.
Oboi.
Fagotti.
Corni in F.
Pianoforte.
Violino I.
Violino II.
Viola.
Violoncello e Basso.
Andante.
I.
cresc.

tr
cresc.

SOLO
p
p
p
mf
mf
mf
mf

Fl.
p
Cor.
a 2.
p
tr
legato
tr

TUTTI
SOLO
legato

tr
p
tr
mf
p
3

p
p
p
tegato
tr
tr
tr

Cor.
tr

TUTTI
tr

SOLO
pp
(Finale, Allegretto.)
Flauto.
Oboi.
Fagotti.
Corni in C.
Trombe in C.
Timpani in C.G.
Pianoforte.
Violino I.
Violino II.
Viola.
Violoncello e Basso.

a 2.

SOLO
a 2.
legato
p
p
p
p

legato
legato
tr

Fl.
Ob.
Fag.
p
p
p
legato

Fl.
Ob.
Fag.
legato
Vcl.
Bassi
staccato
Cor.
p

Ob.
Cor.
Fl.
Ob.
Fag.
Cor.

TUTTI

Fl.
Ob.
Fag.
Cor.
SOLO

legato

Fl.
Ob.
legato
Bassi
Fl.
legato
Vcl.
Ob.
Fag.
legato
Bassi
Fl.
Ob.
Fag.

legato
Fl.
Ob.
Fag.
Cor.
p
legato

Bassi

Fl.
Ob.
Fag.
Fl.
Ob.
TUTTI
f
f
f
f

SOLO
a 2.
f
f
f
3
3
legato
f
f
p
p
p
p
Fl.
p
Ob.
p
Fag.
p

Cor.
p
p
p
p
legato
legato

Ob.
Fag.
legato
Vcl.
Bassi
staccato
Fl.
Ob.
Fag.
legato

Vcl.

Fl.
Ob.
Fag.
legato
TUTTI
SOLO
p
Vcl.

Cor.
legato
Bassi
tr
p
legato

tr
legato
p
legato

tr
tr
Fl.
Ob.
Fag.
sfp
sfp
sfp

p
p
legato
tr
legato

TUTTI
tr
a 2.
f

Piano Concerto No. 26 in D Major, K.537 ("Coronation")

tr
f
a 2.

a 2.

Fl.
Ob.
Fag.
Cor.

p
tr
f
a 2.
SOLO
legato

legato
tr
p
TUTTI
SOLO
Fl.
Ob.
Fag.
Trbe. e Corni
Timp.
f
mfp
fp

p
p
p
p
legato
tr
legato

p
p
p
p
p
p
p
p
legato
3
fp
fp
fp
fp

p
p
p
p
p
p
p
p
tr

tr
3
3
3
legato
fp
legato

TUTTI

a 2.
SOLO
tr

TUTTI
SOLO
f
p

Ob.
Fag.
p
p
p
p
p
p

p
legato

TUTTI
pp
p

Fl.
Ob.
Fag.
Cor.
SOLO
p
p
legato
tr
tr

legato

legato
pp
pp
pp
pp
TUTTI

Ob.
SOLO
Cor.
p
legato
mfp
Fl.
Fag.
fp

fp
fp
fp
fp
p
p
fp
fp
fp
fp
p
tr

TUTTI
a 2.
Cadenza

Larghetto.
SOLO
Flauto.
Oboi.
Fagotti.
Corni in D.
Pianoforte.
Violino I.
Violino II.
Viola.
Violoncello e Basso.
Larghetto.
TUTTI
f
a 2.
tr

SOLO
tr
legato
TUTTI
a 2.
p
f

SOLO
Fag.
a 2.

tr
legato
tr
pp
pp
pp
pp

TUTTI
SOLO
a 2.
tr
TUTTI
SOLO

a 2,
p
pp
pp
pp
pp
Allegretto.
SOLO
Flauto.
Oboi.
Fagotti.
Corni in D.
Trombe in D.
Timpani in D. A.
Pianoforte.
legato
Violino I.
Violino II.
Viola.
Violoncello e Basso.
Allegretto.

TUTTI
SOLO

TUTTI

p
a 2.
f
Vcl.
Bassi
SOLO
legato

Ob.
Fag.
Cor.
I.
legato
Fl.
Ob.
Fag.
Cor.
Trombe

TUTTI
SOLO
Fl.
Ob. a 2.
Fag. a 2.
Cor. a 2.
Tr. a 2.
legato
legato

Fl.
TUTTI
Fag. I.
p
tr
SOLO

Fl.
Ob.
p
p
Fl.
Ob.
Fag.
Cor.
p
legato

p
I.
p
I.
p
legato
Fl.
Ob.
Fag.
fp
fp
fp
fp

Ob.
Fag.
Cor.
p
p
p
tr
legato
fp
fp
fp
fp
Fl.
Ob.
Fag.
Cor.
3
3
3
3

TUTTI
SOLO
Fl.
Ob.
Fag.
Cor.
Trombe
Timp.
legato

TUTTI
SOLO

legato
Fl.
Ob.
Fag.
Cor.
Trombe
TUTTI
SOLO
legato

Fl.
Ob.
Fag.
I.
p
Fl.
Ob.
Fag.
Cor.
p
legato

Fl.
Ob.
Fag.
legato

TUTTI
Fl.
Ob.
Fag.
Cor.
Trombe
Timp.
f
SOLO
legato
p

legato
Ob.
Fag.
TUTTI
p
I.
p
tr
Fl.
Ob.
Fag. I.
p
tr
SOLO

Fl.
Ob.
p
p
p
p
p
p

Fl.
Ob.
Fag.
legato

Ob.
Fag.
p
p
Fl.
p
fp
fp
fp
fp
fp
fp
fp
fp

Ob.
Fag.
Cor.
p
legato
tr
Fl.

Fl.
Ob.
Fag.
legato

TUTTI
SOLO

p
TUTTI
SOLO
TUTTI
SOLO
TUTTI
SOLO
f
f

Fl.
Ob.
Fag.
TUTTI
SOLO
I.
legato
TUTTI
a 2

SOLO
legato
TUTTI
a 2
SOLO

SOLO
TUTTI
a 2.

Piano Concerto No. 27 in B-flat Major, K.595

p
f
mf

mf
p
pp
cresc.
f
a 2.
sf

Fl.
Fag.
Cor.
Fl.
Ob.
Fag.
a 2.
Fl.
Ob.
Fag.
Cor.

p
TUTTI
SOLO
f
legato

TUTTI
SOLO
a 2.

Fl.
Ob.
Fl. TUTTI
Ob.
a 2.
Fag.
a 2.
SOLO
pizz.
pizz.
pizz.
pizz.

Fl.
Ob.
Fag.
p
legato
TUTTI
SOLO
arco
f

TUTTI
SOLO
cresc.
Fl.
Ob.
Fag.
cresc.

TUTTI
SOLO
Vcl.
Bassi
p
cresc.

TUTTI
a 2.
SOLO
Vel.

Ob.
TUTTI
SOLO
TUTTI
Fag.
Bassi
Fl.
SOLO
Ob.
Fag.
legato

Fl.
Ob.
Fag.
Bassi
p

Fl.
Ob.
Cor.
a 2.
Fl.
Ob.
Fag.
p

Ob.
Fag.
TUTTI
p
p
p
p

a 2.
SOLO

legato
TUTTI
SOLO
a 2.
tr
p
f

Fl.
Ob.
Fag.
p
tr
TUTTI
a 2.
f
SOLO
pizz.

Fl.
Ob.
Fag.
p
legato
TUTTI
SOLO
arco
f
mf

p
mf
cresc.
f
Vcl.

TUTTI
SOLO
p
TUTTI
SOLO
TUTTI
SOLO
a2.
sf
tr
Bassi

TUTTI
a 2.
a 2.

Cadenza
tr
f
p

Larghetto.
SOLO
Flauto.
Oboi.
Fagotti.
Corni in Es.
Pianoforte.
Violino I.
Violino II.
Viola.
Violoncello e Basso.
Larghetto.
TUTTI
a2.
cresc.

SOLO
TUTTI
p
f
tr

SOLO
tr
p

p
a 2.
p
p
p

tr
p

Fl.
Cor.
TUTTI

SOLO
p
tr

Allegro.
SOLO
Flauto.
Oboi.
Fagotti.
Corni in B.
Pianoforte.
legato
Violino I.
Violino II.
Viola.
Violoncello e Basso.
Allegro.

TUTTI
SOLO
f
a2.
legato
legato

TUTTI
a 2.

SOLO
p
Vcl.
pp

Bassi

TUTTI
SOLO
f
p

Fl.
TUTTI
SOLO
Ob.
Fag.
p

p
p
p
p
cresc.
cresc.
cresc.
cresc.
cresc.
cresc.
cresc.
cresc.
cresc.
f
f
f
f
f
f
f
f
f

p
legato
TUTTI
f
f
f
a 2.
f
p
p
p
SOLO
f
f
f
f

TUTTI
SOLO
TUTTI
SOLO

a 2.
Vel.
Vel.

Bassi

TUTTI
SOLO

Fl.
Ob.
Fag.
TUTTI
SOLO
p
p

TUTTI
Cad.

SOLO
p
legato
p
p
p
p

TUTTI
a2.
SOLO

p

TUTTI
a2.

Concerto Rondo in D Major, K.382

SOLO
legato
fp
fp
fp
fp
fp
TUTTI
tr
p
SOLO
Fl.
Ob.
Cor.
legato

tr
legato
3
p

TUTTI
tr
p
SOLO

Fl.
Ob.
p
p
tr
Cor.
p
tr

Fl.
Ob.
Cor.
Adagio.
Adagio.

Fl.
Ob.
Cor.
p
p
sfp
sfp
tr

Allegro.
TUTTI
tr
f
p
Allegro.
SOLO

Fl.
Ob.
Cor.

TUTTI
SOLO

TUTTI
SOLO
Tempo I Allegretto grazioso.
Cadenza
pizz.
pizz.
pizz.
TUTTI
tr
pizz.
arco
arco
arco
arco

SOLO
p
p
p
p
f
f
f
f
f
TUTTI
a 2.
f
f
f
f

Cadenzas

Concerto No. 23, 1st Movement

W. A. M. 624.

Concerto No. 27, 1st Movement

sf
tr

Concerto No. 27, 3rd Movement, after first fermata

Concerto No. 27, 3rd Movement, after last fermata

f
p
tr
ff
3